Living Beyond

"WHAT IF?"

Reflection Journal

Dr. Shirley Davis
The Success Doctor™

Living Beyond

"WHAT IF?"

Release the Limits and Realize Your Dreams

REFLECTION JOURNAL
Companion for the book
Living Beyond "WHAT IF?"

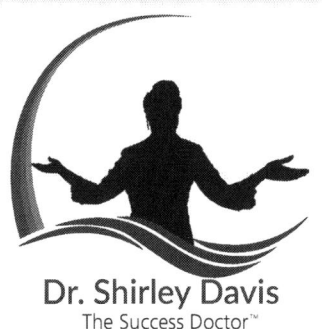

Dr. Shirley Davis
The Success Doctor™

WWW.DRSHIRLEYDAVIS.COM

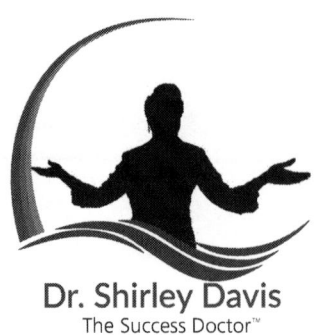

Dr. Shirley Davis
The Success Doctor™

Published by SDS Global Enterprises, Inc.

ISBN: 978-0-9896521-5-5

Request for permission to make copies of any part of this
book can be made to: www.drshirleydavis.com

Content Development & Book Design by Kory Kirby

Companion Book & Theme Song

This reflection journal is the companion to the best selling book "Living Beyond 'What If?': Release the Limits and Realize Your Dreams." It is designed to help you address the self-imposed limiting beliefs that cause you to procrastinate and walk in fear, and that hijack your purpose, power, and possibilities. It will guide you on a journey toward reimagining your life and realizing your dreams by identifying your "why" and developing a Life Plan to stay focused and accountable. It will help you identify the process for creating an Exit Strategy as you close one chapter of your life and enter into a new one. Additionally, it will enable you to adopt the right mindset, establish mutually beneficial relationships, and position you to make better decisions. After working through this journal, you'll be prepared to take more calculated risks by jumping and growing your wings on the way down, and you'll approach life's challenges differently--as new opportunities to learn, grow, and become the best version of yourself. Ultimately, you'll come to understand that there is greatness inside of you and life has a way of bringing it out if you embrace the good, bad and the worst and learn from it to get beyond your What Ifs.

Additional Offerings

At the end of every chapter, you can scan the QR code using your camera and listen to a personalized message from me to you!

Also, on my website you can access a variety of additional resources, merchandise, and bonus materials that will continue to inspire you to be your best!

Reinvent Yourself Bundle

The Seat

Keynotes & Courses

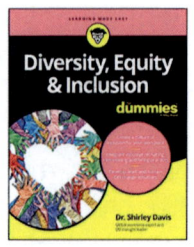

Diversity, Equity & Inclusion for Dummies

Shadow Boxes with Inspirational Quites

How To Use This Journal

 For each chapter I've included key **Reflection Exercises** and questions that are designed to help you do your work - explore the reasons why you aren't living your dreams, remove the limitations, and to lay out a plan to succeed.

 Once you've completed the Reflection Exercises, review the **Action Steps** for implementation and for taking accountability.

This book is dedicated to "The 90%" — those who admit that they are not living their best life because they are chronic procrastinators and are stuck at "What if;" and those who are living with the persistent fears that keep them parked on the side of the road of life and not able to reach their destination.

To all who shared their stories, advice, endorsements, and support this book is dedicated to you.

CONTENTS

This Reflection Journal follows the 8 chapters of my book:

PART 1:

Release the Limits

Chapter 1
Was It Just My Imagination?

> "Imagination is the doorway to unlimited possibilities and key to creating something more meaningful and significant."

In this first chapter we will explore your childhood self. Keeping a diary, or journal has been crucial to my journey. In it, I imagined and wrote down my inner most thoughts and dreams. And as a child nothing seemed impossible. Do you keep a journal? If not, why not? If you do, I encourage you to visit some of your old journal entries and say hello to your past self!

 Reflection Exercises

1. Let's imagine what your life would look like if you had accomplished some of the dreams/goals you had as a child.

What were some activities you enjoyed doing as a child?

_____

_____

_____

_____

_____

_____

Why would you be doing it?

_____

_____

_____

_____

_____

Where would you be living? What places would you have gone?

_____

_____

Who would you be serving?

_____

_____

_____

How would you be feeling?

_____

_____

_____

_____

2. To what extent did you end up accomplishing these things?
   Are you doing any of them today?

_____

_____

_____

_____

_____

_____

_____

_____

_____

_____

_____

When Life Happens and Dreams are Shattered

My life took many twists and turns. I overcame many trials and passed a lot of tests over the years! For these exercises, you will work through some of the life events that shook you to your core and redefined the trajectory of your life.

3. Life Event #1:

What happened?

_____

_____

_____

How did it affect you?

_____

_____

_____

How did you respond?

_____

_____

_____

How did it turn out?

_____

_____

_____

What lessons did you learn?

_____

_____

_____

Finding & Listening to Your Inner Voice

I've discovered that finding and listening to my inner voice to be one of the more important aspects in my life's journey. However, finding, and more importantly listening to my inner voice only developed through deep, reflective work. For the second part of this exercise, journal the questions to each of your four life events:

What were some things that your inner voice was telling you during this event?

_____

_____

_____

_____

What were some things that you wished you had listened to?

_____

_____

_____

_____

What were some things you listened to, you knew to be true and important, but you never did anything about them?

_____

_____

_____

Life Event #2:

What happened?

_____

_____

_____

How did it affect you?

_____

_____

_____

How did you respond?

_____

_____

_____

How did it turn out?

_____

_____

_____

What lessons did you learn?

_____

_____

_____

_____

_____

_____

What were some things that your inner voice was telling you during this event?

_____

_____

_____

_____

_____

_____

What were some things that you wished you had listened to?

_____

_____

_____

_____

_____

What were some things you listened to, you knew to be true and important, but you never did anything about them?

_____

_____

_____

_____

_____

_____

Life Event #3:

What happened?

_____

_____

_____

_____

How did it affect you?

_____

_____

_____

_____

How did you respond?

_____

_____

_____

_____

How did it turn out?

_____

_____

_____

What lessons did you learn?

_____

_____

_____

What were some things that your inner voice was telling you during this event?

_____

_____

_____

_____

What were some things that you wished you had listened to?

_____

_____

_____

_____

What were some things you listened to, you knew to be true and important, but you never did anything about them?

_____

_____

_____

_____

Life Event #4:

What happened?

_____

_____

_____

How did it affect you?

_____

_____

_____

_____

How did you respond?

_____

_____

_____

_____

How did it turn out?

_____

_____

_____

_____

What lessons did you learn?

_____

_____

_____

_____

What were some things that your inner voice was telling you during this event?

_____

_____

_____

_____

_____

What were some things that you wished you had listened to?

_____

_____

_____

_____

_____

What were some things you listened to, you knew to be true and important, but you never did anything about them?

_____

_____

_____

_____

_____

_____

_____

_____

6. What was an experience in your young life that brought everything you knew into question? In other words, list a defining moment.

_____

_____

_____

_____

_____

_____

_____

_____

7. Think back to a time when you came face to face with yourself. How did this situation allow you to find new inner strength?

_____

_____

_____

_____

_____

_____

_____

_____

_____

8. Recognizing flaws in yourself requires hard work. But once you do, you can work with them, instead of them working against you. What are some of your flaws that have paralyzed you from moving forward?

_____

_____

_____

_____

_____

_____

_____

9. How will acknowledging these flaws help you in the long run?

_____

_____

_____

_____

_____

_____

_____

_____

_____

_____

 # Chapter 1 Action Steps: Taking Accountability

> "I had to get out of my own way so that I could start living the life that I was destined to live."

Here begins my journey:

- *I had to embark on a journey of self-development in order to get to self-actualization.*
- *I had to accept that I had a painful past.*
- *I needed to learn, grow, and expel the self-imposed limits that I had internalized.*
- *I needed to take 100% accountability for my life.*

Taking accountability is actually one of my key action steps to success!

What do you need to take accountability for?

- A financial situation?
- Past experiences?
- Lack of education?
- Self-limiting beliefs?
- Staying at a terrible job?
- Bad Relationships?

_____

_____

_____

_____

What have you learned? What do you wish you had done differently?

_____

_____

_____

_____

In this chapter you will explore some of the main reasons that you procrastinate and identify what you keep procrastinating on. You will also learn some steps for how to move from being a procrastinator to a producer.

 **Reflection Exercises**

1. Are you living your best life? Or are you one of the 90% that are not living their dreams? Why or why not?

_____

_____

_____

_____

_____

_____

_____

2. What are you putting off right now that needs to be done?

_____

_____

_____

_____

_____

_____

_____

_____

3. What are the biggest distractions that keep you from doing what you know you should do?

_____

_____

_____

_____

_____

_____

_____

_____

4. What are some of the things that take up most of your time?

_____

_____

_____

_____

_____

_____

_____

_____

_____

_____

5. Present bias is when we settle for a smaller present reward rather than wait for a larger future reward. Can you think of any smaller present rewards that you are currently settling for, instead of waiting for a larger future reward?

Why We Procrastinate -
Your Present Self vs Your Future Self

James Clear, the New York Times best-selling author of **Atomic Habits,** *explains "time inconsistency" and procrastination as the tendency of the human brain to value immediate rewards more highly than future rewards. When you set goals for yourself you are actually making plans for your Future Self. The Future Self values long-term goals. While the Future Self can set goals, only the Present Self can take action. Researchers have discovered that the Present Self really likes instant gratification, not long-term payoffs.*

Your Present Self

6. What does your Present Self look and feel like? Be specific.

My present self looks like....   *My present self feels like....*

_____   _____

_____   _____

_____   _____

_____   _____

_____   _____

_____   _____

_____   _____

_____   _____

Your Future Self

7. What does your Future Self look and feel like? Be specific.

My future self looks like....   *My future self feels like....*

_____   _____

_____   _____

_____   _____

_____   _____

_____   _____

_____   _____

_____   _____

8. What should your Present Self be doing, to *look* and *feel* like your Future Self?

_____

_____

_____

_____

_____

_____

_____

_____

_____

_____

_____

Big Goals Need Small Steps

I used to write out goals and if they were too big, I would procrastinate because I didn't feel I had time to complete them. Now I approach goals in smaller steps. I do something every day that gets me closer to reaching my goals. No matter how small.

9. Write one big goal of yours. Then, break that goal down in smaller steps. And from there, even smaller steps, until you get to a leading task (tasks that are quick and easy and don't require much thought). Write out 3-4 leading tasks you can do tomorrow, that will get you closer to reaching your goal.

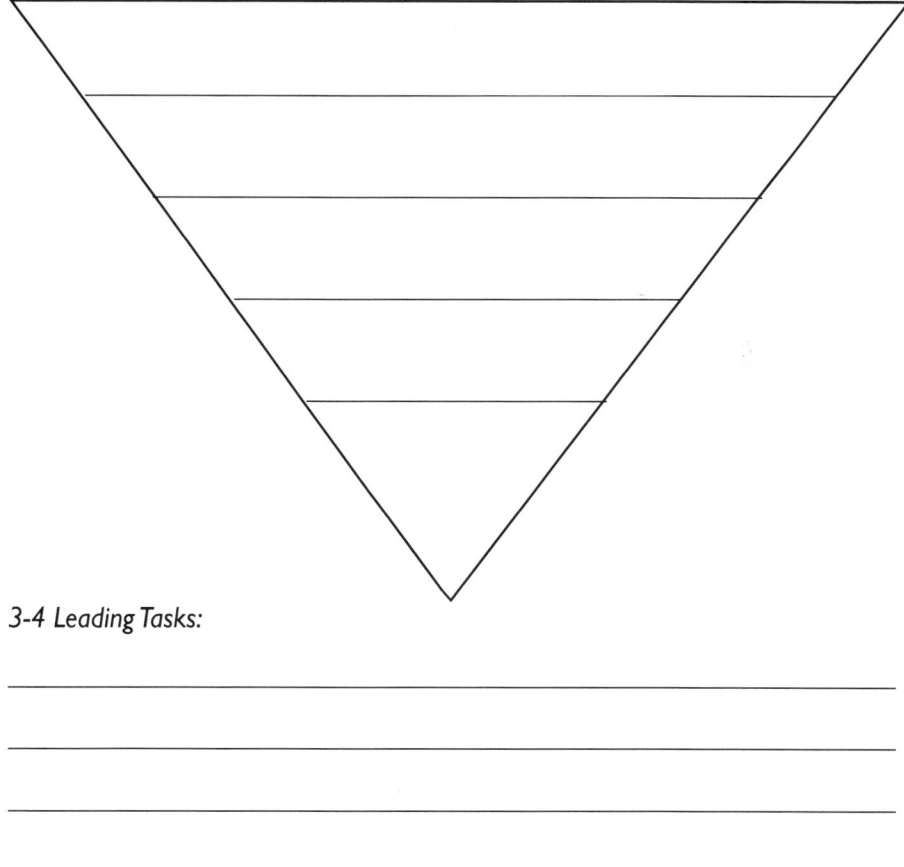

3-4 Leading Tasks:

_____

_____

_____

_____

Your Daily Routine

10. For this exercise review your daily routine, list it below, and then allocate that time for your first few leading tasks that you listed on the previous page.

Morning Routine

_____

_____

_____

_____

_____

_____

_____

_____

Afternoon Routine

_____

_____

_____

_____

_____

_____

_____

_____

_____

_____

Evening Routine

_____

_____

_____

_____

_____

_____

_____

_____

_____

Return to this exercise and repeat as needed. Also, be sure to check in on your goals consistently (I do it at least monthly) to ensure you are staying on track. This is an important step that I can't stress enough. You have to adjust your goals as needed, because life happens and unexpected disruptions come that may require you to shift your timeline for completion.

What Do You Procrastinate On The Most?

When I decided to write this book, I took a personal inventory of the things I've been most guilty of procrastinating on over the years. Here are a few of mine: going to the gym, homework, paying bills, returning phone calls, completing home projects, car repairs, learning a new language, starting a business, writing a book, and ending a bad relationship.

11. For this exercise take a personal inventory of the things you are most guilty of procrastinating on and list them below.

1. _____

2. _____

3. _____

4. _____

5. _____

6. _____

7. _____

8. _____

9. _____

10. _____

_____

_____

_____

_____

12. Study this list you have made and begin to think about the consequences of the tasks you have been guilty of procrastinating on most over the years. What are these consequences?

_____

_____

_____

_____

_____

_____

_____

13. Which are tied directly to realizing your dreams? More important, ask yourself, "Why do I keep procrastinating, and how can I stop?

_____

_____

_____

_____

_____

_____

_____

_____

_____

_____

Chapter 2 Action Steps:
Move from Being a Procrastinator
to Being a Producer

"When we release the limitations of procrastination, a world opens up that produces new possibilities, new opportunities, and new strategies for realizing our dreams."

The Next Time You Find Yourself Procrastinating Ask Yourself the Following Questions:

1. If I procrastinate, what will it cost me? If I get it done, what is the reward?

2. Do I have the capacity, competence, and ability to do it?

3. Am I passionate about this task?

4. Are any guilt and shame driving my procrastination?

5. Am I overwhelmed by the process of changing?

6. If not now, when? If not me, who?

7. What am I trying to avoid by not completing the task?

8. How does putting off this task or decision make me feel?

How to Move from Being a Procrastinator to Being a Producer:

Confront the reasons you procrastinate.

Set realistic goals.

Break your goals into smaller, more manageable tasks (remember leading tasks).

Think outside the box and find a creative way that works for you.

Remove limitations that you have placed on yourself.

Check in on your goals consistently
(do it at least monthly).

Identify a few trusted friends who will hold you accountable. Tell them your goal or dream and when you plan to accomplish it, and allow them to check in on your progress.

And lastly, always remember: Procrastination is not a static condition. It comes down to deciding, committing, and acting. It's a daily fight and it's not easy, but we have the power to move from being a procrastinator to being a producer.

Scan this QR code to listen to a personal message from me.

Chapter 3
Stuck On "What If?"
Common Disempowering Questions

"If we are serious about releasing the limits that keep us from realizing our dreams, we must start by exposing the questions that come from the negative thoughts, stories, and self-talk that we believe about ourselves."

In this chapter you will uncover some of your most common limiting beliefs that you've put on yourself and that you've allowed to derail your purpose, passion, and possibilities.

 **Reflection Exercises**

1. What are some "What if" questions that you regularly face?

   Questions that derail your **PURPOSE**:

   _____

   _____

   _____

   _____

   _____

   Questions that derail your **PASSION:**

   _____

   _____

   _____

   _____

   _____

   Questions that derail your **POSSIBILITIES:**

   _____

   _____

   _____

   _____

"What If" Questions

Below is a list of common disempowering "What if" questions. Review the list and place a checkmark in the ones you keep believing and speaking to yourself. Consider how each resonates in your professional and your personal life.

- [ ] What if I'm not good enough?
- [ ] What if I'm not attractive enough?
- [ ] What if I don't have enough money?
- [ ] What if I'm not smart enough?
- [ ] What if I get rejected or not selected?
- [ ] What if I get fired?
- [ ] What if I fail?
- [ ] What if I say the wrong thing?
- [ ] What if I am not qualified?
- [ ] What if I don't have time?
- [ ] What if I look stupid?
- [ ] What if my heart gets broken?
- [ ] What if others won't like me?
- [ ] What if I'm too old (or too young)?
- [ ] What if I succeed, then what?

2. Next, revisit those 4 major life events that you listed in Chapter 1. Were you asking yourself any of these "What if" questions during these events?

_____

_____

_____

_____

3. Have you ever asked your supervisor what it would take to get promoted or to move to the next level? If yes, reflect on that experience. How did it go? If not, why haven't you?

_____

_____

_____

_____

_____

_____

_____

4. What additional education or certifications would you like to obtain?

- _____   - _____

- _____   - _____

- _____   - _____

- _____   - _____

- _____   - _____

5. What kind of books do you need to read or what kind of podcast do you need to listen to?

- _____

- _____

- _____

- _____

- _____

6. What kind of mentor would you like?

- _____

- _____

- _____

- _____

- _____

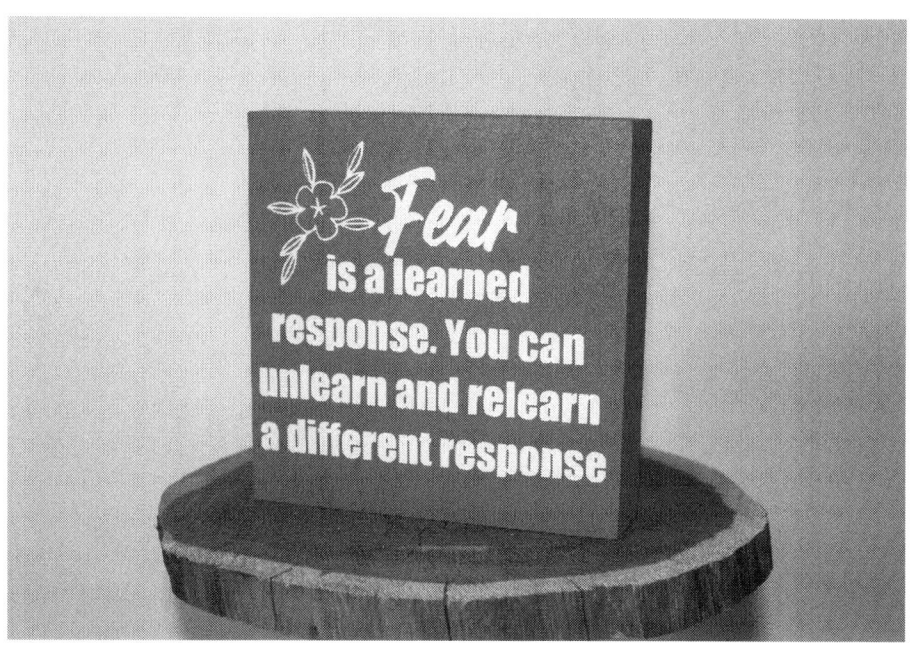

7. What would you do if you knew you couldn't fail?

_____

_____

_____

_____

_____

8. Do you compare yourself to others? In what way?

_____

_____

_____

_____

_____

_____

9. How does your current self, compare to your past self?

Current Self	Past Self

10. Are you getting wiser and stronger from every experience? Or are you getting bitter and resentful from the challenges you've faced? Explain.

_____

_____

_____

_____

_____

_____

_____

_____

11. What assumptions are holding you back from achieving your dreams and goals?

_____

_____

_____

_____

_____

_____

_____

_____

_____

_____

_____

_____

Take Inventory of Your Strengths and Positive Traits

12. Instead of drowning in self-doubt, and disempowering "What if" questions, take inventory of your strengths and positive traits by listing them out below. For each strength or trait, write out how you can enhance them to become better every day.

Strength: _____

Ways to Enhance: _____

_____

Strength: _____

Ways to Enhance: _____

_____

Strength: _____

Ways to Enhance: _____

_____

Strength: _____

Ways to Enhance: _____

_____

Strength: _____

Ways to Enhance: _____

_____

Strength: _____

Ways to Enhance: _____

_____

Developing the Right Attitude Toward Failure

Failure is a part of the process of living. To live the life we've imagined, we must confront the fear of failure and even failure itself. Many of us may have been taught that failure is not an option. Failure can be an option as long as we recognize that failure isn't final, that it isn't forever. We need to learn from our failures, learn from our mistakes, and not be afraid to get back up. Failing doesn't mean you've reached the end of the road. You can use it as a springboard to the next level of your life.

13. List three failures or mistakes you've made that were transformative. What did you learn from them?

Failure/Mistake: _____

_____

Lesson: _____

_____

Failure/Mistake: _____

_____

Lesson: _____

_____

Failure/Mistake: _____

_____

Lesson: _____

_____

14. How can you use what you learned to springboard you to the next level of your life?

_____

_____

_____

_____

_____

_____

_____

_____

_____

_____

_____

_____

Overcoming Rejections

I remember getting rejected for a position that I thought for sure I should have been hired for. Sometime later I was offered a better opportunity (more money, better benefits, and a better work environment). I began to believe that things happen for a reason, and even though we don't always understand why things happen, over time they have a way of working out a better outcome.

15. Think of a time in your life when a rejection ultimately resulted in a better outcome.

_____

_____

_____

_____

_____

_____

16. Do you believe that all things happen for a reason? Give an example.

_____

_____

_____

_____

_____

_____

_____

Chapter 3 Action Steps: Debunking/Dismantling Disempowering Beliefs

> "Our beliefs must change with the times; they must also change alongside our goals."

One of the exercises that became a ritual in my journey to get beyond my "What if?" questions was listing the most common disempowering questions that would keep me stuck and then countering them with empowering responses I would actually say to myself as affirmations. I invite you to start with three to focus on this week until your language changes.

Then select three more empowering responses the following week, and three more the week after that, until you have identified and debunked every disempowering question that derails your destiny. Make a commitment to reprogram your mind to have an empowering response for every one of them.

Examples of Disempowering "What if's" and Their Empowering Responses

Place a check mark beside those "What If" questions that you keep asking yourself. Then begin to use the Empowering Responses as your affirmations. Feel free to add to those responses.

Disempowering "What If?" Questions	Empowering Responses
☐ What if I'm not good enough?	I am unique and special. There is greatness inside of me and I have something of value to offer. I will give it my best and continue to grow. If someone doesn't think I'm good enough, it's only their opinion. Most important, it's about how I feel about me, and I AM good enough.
☐ What if I don't have enough money?	This is a temporary state. Money is a resource, but it doesn't define who I am. I am on a financial manage- ment plan to save, increase my income, and one day finance my dreams.
☐ What if I'm not smart enough?	What I don't know now I am open to learning. I am a lifelong learner who will continue to educate myself.
☐ What if I get rejected or not selected?	Things happen for a reason. This was not the right opportunity or the right person, so a better one is around the corner. I won't stop trying because what one person may not see in me many more will.

Disempowering "What If?" Questions	Empowering Responses
☐ What if I get fired?	I would be released to pursue new opportunities. Everything has an expiration date, so it must have been time to move on. When I ask or do something that is based on my personal conviction, I won't be afraid of the consequences. Better opportunities will come along.
☐ What if I fail?	Failure is a part of life but it's not the end of the world. I will keep trying and I will learn from the experiences and be better the next time.
☐ What if I look stupid?	I'm going to give it my best shot and be proud that I tried.

Try writing some of your own...

_____   _____

_____   _____

_____

_____

_____   _____

_____   _____

_____

Overcoming Our Disempowering Beliefs Isn't Easy

Overcoming our disempowering beliefs takes a significant amount of work, introspection, and time. Moreover, it isn't a "one and done." You don't just go through this process once and be finished with it. Rather, it's an ongoing process of steps we must revisit over and over. We must therefore commit ourselves to long-term change, and our beliefs are of course at the core of that transformation. They are the foundation of who we are. Remember, the beliefs that got you to where you are today won't get you to where you want to be tomorrow. They influence every aspect of your life. Don't let your beliefs prevent you from living that life you've always imagined.

Scan this QR code to listen to a
personal message from me.

Chapter 4
Face Your Fears Head On

"We are either living our fears or living our dreams."

In this chapter, you identify your fears and learn ways to confront them and put them behind you.

Reflection Exercises

1. What does fear mean to you?

_____

_____

_____

_____

2. What do you fear? Why?

_____

_____

_____

_____

3. How has it affected your dreams and your future?

_____

_____

_____

_____

_____

_____

_____

_____

Don't live your fears, live your dreams

4. On a scale of 1 to 10, circle how ready you are to confront your fears.

(1 = not ready at all; 10 = completely ready).

○   ○   ○   ○   ○   ○   ○   ○   ○   ○
1   2   3   4   5   6   7   8   9   10

Explain

_____

_____

5. What are some fears that you would like to conquer?

- _____
- _____
- _____
- _____
- _____
- _____
- _____

6. What are some fears that you're willing to live with?

_____

_____

_____

_____

_____

_____

The Golden Cage

Walking and living in fear can cause us to create what I call a Golden Cage. We use this cage as a safety mechanism that protects us from the world but also blocks others out. If we stay in that cage too long, it gets comfortable and familiar. We can even start to accessorize our cage so that it looks and feels pretty and comfortable to live in. And even though we feel safe and the cage is all dressed up, we don't realize that we are isolating ourselves from others and creating self-imposed limitations that keep us from living our best life.

For this exercise, I'd like you to openly journal on the following questions:

7. Have you built a Golden Cage and accessorized it to be your comfort zone? How?

_____

_____

_____

_____

_____

_____

_____

_____

_____

_____

_____

_____

_____

8. Are you giving voice to those negative, self-defeating, lifelimiting questions? Explain.

○ Yes   ○ No

_____

_____

_____

_____

9. Are you shutting yourself off from others who want to help you? Why? What are you afraid of?

○ Yes   ○ No

_____

_____

_____

_____

10. Are you isolating yourself from reality because the pain of your past makes it too hard to face your future?

○ Yes   ○ No

_____

_____

_____

_____

11. Are you living or just existing?

○ Living!   ○ Existing

Because of Fear, I...

12. In the statements below place a checkmark beside those that apply to you:

    ☐ Because of fear, I stayed at jobs far beyond my expiration date.

    ☐ Because of fear, I've vacated many great ideas— ideas that could have impacted someone else's life but I talked myself out of them because of fear.

    ☐ Because of fear, I could have launched my own business a decade ago, and been successful, but I was afraid it would fail, and I would be in more debt as a result.

    ☐ Because of fear, I've avoided getting involved in relationships because I was afraid they might be another abusive, toxic, or unhealthy situation.

13. For this exercise, repeat what I did above by writing out, "Because of fear, I"... and then list a few things you've also done because of fear.

_____

_____

_____

_____

_____

_____

_____

Learning Through Facing Fear

I faced my fear of a bully by confronting her head on and defending myself. I learned a few lessons from that incident that followed me into my adult life. First, when I was fearful, I didn't realize my own strength until I had to come face to face with my insecurities and inadequacies. Second, had I not stood up to that fear (the bully), the torment would have continued. In other words, you cannot conquer what you aren't willing to confront. Third, when faced with fear, it may not be as big and as bad as it appears. It may just be sounding off a lot of noise but not be able to overtake you.

14. Based on the fears you just listed, write down a time you faced one of your fears. Then write out three lessons you learned from that experience.

_____

_____

_____

_____

_____

_____

_____

_____

_____

_____

_____

_____

_____

_____

 **Chapter 4 Action Steps:**
Take the Power Out of Your Fears

When I took on another job or decided to leave a bad relationship, I wrote down every bad thing that could happen, then listed how they would affect me. Beside every fear I listed some strategies for how to respond. Doing this exercise took the power out of the fears I had, and I felt more in control. Turns out that most of the things I worried about never happened anyway.

Next time you are faced with a big decision like switching jobs, or leaving a relationship, consider these 3 tips:

1. Write down every bad thing that could happen.
2. List how these things would affect you.
3. List strategies for how to respond to these things.

Once you make the decision, and face the fear, reflect:

1. Did any of the "bad things" happen?
2. If they did, was it as bad or worse as you thought?

Six Steps for Facing Your Fears Head On

1. **SHIFT** your thinking and your attitude about your fears by acknowledging them. Learn that what you resist will persist, and that you cannot conquer what you are not willing to confront. Recognize that fears are a normal part of life, and everyone has them.

2. **ASK** a lot of questions and seek to dismantle your fears by seeking reassurances.

3. **JUMP** out there and give it a try. Decide not to be paralyzed by fear. Face one fear at a time. Don't overwhelm yourself by trying to conquer too much too fast. Take baby steps but do step out. And when you falter, immediately try again before fear sets back in.

4. **BUILD** up your self-confidence and sense of self-worth by speaking positive and empowering affirmations. There is power in our words, and we can use them to build up instead of tear down. When you feel fear, choose to calm down and not panic.

5. **WRITE** down each fear as you conquer them and use it as a testimonial to recall for the next fear you need to face.

6. **IMAGINE** your dreams becoming reality. Learn to see yourself beyond your fear and think of the best-case scenario instead of dwelling on the worst-case scenario.

Scan this QR code to listen to a personal message from me.

PART 2:

Realize Your Dreams

Chapter 5
In Search of Significance

"If you truly know why you were born and how gifted and talented and valuable you are, then you have to believe there's nothing you can't achieve."

In this chapter, you will learn ways to identify and set achievable goals for your life.

Reflection Exercises

1. What are some of the common New Year's Resolutions you set each year?

_____

_____

_____

_____

_____

_____

_____

2. Have you been successful in achieving your resolutions?

_____

_____

_____

_____

_____

_____

_____

_____

_____

List those you achieved, and those you did not achieve. Then detail why you didn't achieve them.

Achieved	Not Achieved

Why?

_____

_____

_____

3. According to U.S. News and World Report, more than 40% of us make resolutions, and at the end of the year only 8% of us feel we were successful in achieving our goals. In fact, on average, 80% of resolutions fail by the second week of February each year. Why do you think this is the case?

_____

_____

_____

_____

_____

_____

4. At the end of each year, how can you carve out some time alone to process, reflect, and re-group? (In my book, I call it a "METREAT"™)

_____

_____

_____

_____

5. What would this "METREAT"™ look like for you?

_____

_____

_____

_____

_____

_____

_____

6. What are some of the hopes and dreams that you still want to accomplish?

_____

_____

_____

_____

_____

_____

_____

Take Inventory of Where You Are

So often we go through life without slowing down to take inventory of where we are, to count our blessings, smell the flowers, and celebrate our milestones. When we don't do this, we allow so much time to pass and we forget about the things we've accomplished and all that has happened in our life. Doing this review helps us to offset some of the challenges we face, including some of the bad things that can overshadow our dreams and aspirations.

7. Take an inventory of where you are. Write down all of the accomplishments from the past year(s) that you are proud of.

_____

_____

_____

_____

_____

_____

_____

_____

_____

_____

_____

_____

_____

8. What are some of your life-goals. Write them down below. Have any been completed? Not completed? Why?

_____

_____

_____

_____

_____

_____

9. Determine which goals you would like to keep pursuing, and which goals can be abandoned altogether.

_____

_____

_____

_____

_____

_____

_____

Understanding Your Purpose

In this exercise you will write out your purpose statement. But first, you need to understand that your purpose starts with the most basic questions in life:

Who am I? Why am I here?

When you start answering these questions you'll bring new meaning to every aspect of your life—to your career, to your relationships, and to your responses to life's challenges.

10. Who am I?

_____

_____

_____

_____

_____

_____

_____

11. Why am I here?

_____

_____

_____

_____

_____

_____

_____

Purpose is what you were created and born to do. It's your why. It's the reason you're wired the way you are. It's the reason you possess the kinds of skills and talents you have. Purpose has to do with your destiny (or your destination). It drives you and makes you get out of bed every morning. It gives you a strong sense of self-worth and a dose of energy and passion for life. And it guides your choices and decisions. I believe you have no limitations except the ones you have accepted from others and those that you have imposed on yourself. If you truly know why you were born and how gifted and talented and valuable you are, then you have to believe there's nothing you can't achieve.

12. How are your life experiences preparing you for what you are destined to achieve?

_____

_____

_____

_____

_____

_____

_____

_____

_____

_____

_____

_____

_____

_____

My purpose statement is to train, coach, teach, and empower others with knowledge, strategies, and skills, and to enable them to see a larger vision for themselves so that they find meaning, fulfillment, and success in every area of their life.

13. What's your purpose statement?

_____

_____

_____

_____

_____

_____

_____

_____

_____

_____

_____

_____

_____

_____

_____

_____

How to Develop Your Life Plan

In this exercise you will be developing your Life Plan: a written outline of the visions, dreams, and goals you want to accomplish within a certain time frame.

It documents your purpose and priorities and provides a clear path for decision-making. It also brings your thoughts to life and manifests your dreams. A major consideration in creating a Life Plan is to remain flexible and make it a living, breathing document that is updated according to how your life changes and as you evolve and mature. Just like a phone app that can prompt you to do things, or like a GPS that gives you directions, so does a Life Plan. It is important to write down your plan, because a written plan is easier to remember, helps you to stay focused, and frees your mind to focus on other things.

Developing your Life Plan consists of 5 main steps:

STEP 1: Identifying Your Categories of Goals

Develop the categories of goals for your Life Plan. For example here are mine:

(1) Career/professional

(2) Health/wellness

(3) Personal relationships/home life

(4) Finances

(5) Spirituality

My career goals have included working toward a higher position, completing a certification, or applying for a promotion; and my financial goals have included saving a certain amount of money, paying off certain bills, or giving more money to charities.

15. List your categories of goals for your Life Plan.

(1) _____

(2) _____

(3) _____

(4) _____

(5) _____

STEP 2: Performing a Self Assessment

Take a self-assessment of where you are (feel free to re-visit Reflection Exercise: Take Inventory of Where You Are earlier in the chapter.) This assessment requires you to be open, authentic, and honest with yourself. You have to be willing to call out your areas that need improvement, your fatal flaws, and your failures.

I know it's easy to list your strengths and focus on them, but when you don't grow and develop new skill sets, mindsets, attitudes, and behaviors, you can become obsolete and complacent. This assessment should be focused on avoiding complacency in your life.

Consider the following questions to help with this self-assessment:

16. What do you need to improve on?

_____

_____

_____

_____

_____

17. What are your fatal flaws?

_____

_____

_____

_____

_____

_____

18. What are some of your biggest failures?

_____

_____

_____

_____

_____

_____

What did you learn from these failures?

_____

_____

_____

_____

_____

_____

19. What new skills do you need to learn?

_____

_____

_____

_____

_____

_____

20. How could you benefit from a mindset shift?

_____

_____

_____

_____

_____

_____

21. Are there any bad behaviors or habits you want to change?

_____

_____

_____

_____

_____

_____

STEP 3: Identifying Your Core Values

When you are faced with decisions, you can measure your options against your values and choose the option that best aligns with your priorities or that moves you forward toward realizing your dreams. Sticking to your core values can also help you deprioritize things that take up a lot of your time but have no relationship to your purpose. In other words, it will give you a reason to say no.

Examples of core values include integrity, honesty, respect, family, loyalty, commitment, authenticity, and spirituality.

22. What are your core values?

- _____

- _____

- _____

- _____

- _____

STEP 4: Creating Long, Mid, and Short-Term Goals

The next step for creating your Life Plan is to think long-term, mid-term, and short-term. Identify where you see yourself in ten years, five years, and one to three years. Then list your overall goal for what you want to achieve in one year and the most important tasks that will get you there. Break up those tasks by quarter, then by month, then by week.

23. Where do you see yourself in 10 years?

_____

_____

_____

_____

_____

...in 5 years?

_____

_____

_____

_____

...in 1-3 years?

_____

_____

_____

_____

24. What is your overall goal for one year?

_____

_____

_____

_____

_____

_____

What are your quarterly tasks to achieve this goal?

_____

_____

_____

_____

_____

What are your monthly tasks to achieve this goal?

_____

_____

_____

_____

_____

_____

What are your weekly tasks to achieve this goal?

_____

_____

_____

_____

_____

_____

_____

STEP 5: Identifying Milestones and What Success Will Look Like

The last thing to be included in your Life Plan is specific milestones and what success looks like to you. This way you have a means to measure your progress along the way.

25. List the specific milestones to achieving your goals.

_____

_____

_____

_____

_____

26. What will success look like?

_____

_____

_____

_____

Your Life Plan

In the space below, write out your Life Plan. All in all your Life Plan will be a concise paragraph that consists of:
1. Your categories of goals
2. A self-assessment
3. Your core values
4. Long-term, mid-term, and short-term goals
5. Specific milestones and your own definition of success

_____

_____

_____

_____

_____

_____

_____

_____

_____

_____

_____

_____

_____

_____

_____

_____

_____

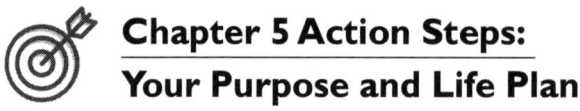 **Chapter 5 Action Steps:**
Your Purpose and Life Plan

Over the next 30-60 days refine your purpose statement. Once you are clear on your purpose, devise your Life Plan and share it with someone who knows you well and that you trust so that you can solicit feedback and additional suggestions.

Takeaways

1. My purpose and Life Plan are at the backbone of my success. Being clear, and concise with these two items are really important.
2. Be willing to confront your own insecurities, short comings, and limitations that keep you from discovering your purpose & Life Plan.
3. Challenge your beliefs that keep you asking "What If?"
4. Remember, this is an investment into your personal success and you are worth the investment!

Scan this QR code to listen to a personal message from me.

Chapter 6
Relationships Are The New Currency

"Good relationships are the foundation for success in all areas of life."

In this chapter you will examine your current relationships and identify new relationships that will help you live your purpose.

 Reflection Exercises

1. Practicing self-care isn't selfish, it's crucial so you can feel your best, do your best work, and achieve your dreams. How do you practice self-care?

_____

_____

_____

_____

_____

_____

2. What does a healthy relationship look like to you?

_____

_____

_____

_____

_____

_____

_____

_____

_____

3. Describe the kind of relationship that you have with yourself.

_____

_____

_____

_____

_____

_____

How Do You Really Know You Love Yourself?

Having been through the process of self-development and overcoming self-defeating beliefs, I offer here a few ways to know if you are in a great relationship with yourself. Some of these statements were shared by many of my mentors and advisers who experienced similar journeys toward self-love.

4. Review the following list and check all the statements that are true about you.

    ☐ You are true to yourself (meaning you are honest with yourself about where you are in life and about your strengths, shortcomings, needs, hurts, feelings, and so on).

    ☐ You accept your flaws and your mistakes, and you don't dwell on them.

    ☐ You are kind to others.

    ☐ You don't seek validation from external sources, such as social media.

    ☐ You value your alone time.

    ☐ You celebrate yourself.

    ☐ You take care of your mental and physical health.

    ☐ You manage your finances responsibly.

    ☐ You have a positive attitude.

    ☐ You are grateful for what you have.

5. Which of these do you need to work on?

    _____

    _____

    _____

Your Personal Board of Advisors

My personal board of advisers are my closest and most trusted family members, friends, and colleagues. My board of advisers has built me up, pushed me forward, made me better, and provided the kind of support that has enabled me to realize my dreams. They know how I think and what my strengths and weaknesses are, so they know how to support me personally and professionally. Through the years, they have been instrumental in my growth, my recovery from failures, and my reinvention.

6. Think about who is (would) be on your personal board of advisors? Who are your most trusted family members, friends, and colleagues?

Who?	Why?

Building an Extended, Diverse Network

I have an extended network that provides me great counsel and wisdom from their experience, and they share resources that help me in my career and business endeavors. It has been said that it's not what you know, it's who you know, and this couldn't be a truer reason for having a network. I consider myself a master connector and an effective relationship builder, and I have experienced the value that having a great network can bring.

7. Do you have a diverse network?

○   ○
Yes   No

8. What are some of the benefits of having a broad, diverse network that you've enjoyed?

- _____
- _____
- _____
- _____
- _____
- _____

If your network is not as diverse as it could be, use the following three strategies to help build it:

Strategy 1: Assess your current network.
When answering the following questions, consider whether your network differs in:

Race/Ethnicity	Ages	Thinking Style
Gender	Beliefs	Location
Cultures	Personalities	Religion/ Spirituality
Experiences	Skill Sets	Communication

Remember, it's about quality over quantity. Once you have answered and considered these questions, you will have a better idea of who you already have and who else you need to invite into your network.

8. Who are the people currently in your network?

_____

_____

_____

_____

_____

9. Why did you select them, or vice versa?

_____

_____

_____

_____

10. What skills, experience, and resources do they offer?

_____

_____

_____

_____

_____

11. Does everyone in your network look, think, and act like you?

_____

_____

_____

_____

_____

Strategy 2: Initiate Conversations

While attending live social events such as conferences, conventions, seminars, or workshops, I do this often. Here's the approach I take. Let's say you're at the conference reception or at a table for lunch or sitting beside someone in a session. Take the first step and initiate a conversation. Get to know who they are, what they do, and about their experiences and expertise.

Do you struggle to "go first," and initiate conversations? If so, revisit some of the work you did in Chapter 4 on Facing Your Fears Head On.

Strategy 3: Connect Online

I conduct searches via social media sites (LinkedIn, Twitter, Instagram, Facebook, etc.), along with other Internet searches to find professionals who share my interests and have unique skills and expertise that I can benefit from, and I invite them to connect. Also, when I come across someone's online post that interests me, I engage with them by responding and thanking them for their posts. Then I send them an invitation to connect, stating that I like to learn from interesting people like them and would like to add them to my network.

12. What are some ways that you can expand your social media connections?

_____

_____

_____

_____

_____

Chapter 6 Action Steps:
Relationships are the New Currency

Identify ways to foster and optimize better relationships with:
Self
Personal Board of Advisors
Broad/Extended Diverse Network

Takeaway

Over the years I have learned that people hire, promote, pay more, and do business with people they know, like, and trust. I often say that it's not just what you know or who you know but what they know about you. Having a loving relationship with yourself and learning the art of building beneficial relationships, as well as knowing how to leverage those relationships in a way that helps you learn, grow, and become better, are critical ingredients in achieving your dreams.

Scan this QR code to listen to a
personal message from me.

Chapter 7
Jump and Grow Your Wings on the Way Down

"Life's most rewarding experiences comes as a result of taking risks on yourself and your dreams and believing that those risks are worth taking."

In this chapter you will examine ways to take calculated risks that will get you closer to living your dreams.

 **Reflection Exercises**

1. What does, *"jump and grow your wings on the way down,"* mean to you?

_____

_____

_____

_____

_____

_____

_____

_____

2. What are a few things you would like to do, but are afraid of jumping into?

_____

_____

_____

_____

_____

_____

3. Why does it feel risky to you to jump?

_____

_____

_____

_____

_____

4. What's holding you back from jumping towards your goals?

_____

_____

_____

_____

_____

Jump and Grow Your Wings on the Way Down

We've all inevitably had to make some jumps in our lives. For this exercise, please reflect on a few of these questions.

5. Have you ever jumped and done something outside of your comfort zone?

_____

_____

_____

6. How did you feel?

_____

_____

_____

_____

_____

7. Was the jump as scary as you thought it would be?

_____

_____

8. Did all your worst fears come true?

_____

_____

_____

9. What went wrong?

_____

_____

_____

_____

_____

10. What went right?

_____

_____

_____

_____

11. What did you learn, or in other words, did you grow your wings on the way down?

_____

_____

_____

_____

_____

_____

_____

Planning to Jump and Grow Your Wings on the Way Down

Write out something that you would like to jump into within in the next 12 months. For example, I jumped and resigned from my job; I jumped and left a bad relationship; I jumped and launched my global consulting firm; I jumped and wrote my first book; I jumped and moved to a place I had never visited.

12. I'd to like to jump and...

_____

_____

_____

_____

_____

Remember, you don't have to jump all at once. You can continue doing what you're doing, and simply take baby steps over time.

13. Next, create a list of all the "What if?" questions and all the things you fear about this jump.

What if....

- _____
- _____
- _____
- _____
- _____
- _____
- _____
- _____

14. Now create another list of how to overcome each of these.

- _____
- _____
- _____
- _____
- _____
- _____
- _____
- _____

15. And finally, write down your vision statement for this jump so that you have clarity and can stay focused on the goal.

_____

_____

_____

_____

_____

_____

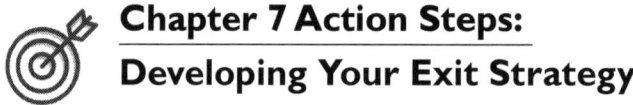

Chapter 7 Action Steps: Developing Your Exit Strategy

Simply put, an exit strategy is a plan or road map for leaving your current situation and entering into your next chapter. It lays out the steps and strategies for how you will make the transition. It should also detail the financial implications, potential risks, and associated obstacles, as well as the expected outcomes and tangible benefits. For example, when I wanted to move from one type of position to another in the same company, I created a well thought-out exit strategy:

How I Developed My Exit Strategy:

Step 1   I identified where I wanted to be in the near future (what was my next chapter) and what success would look like. I also got clear about my WHY.

Step 2   I did my homework. I found out what specific requirements, skills, resources and qualifications would be needed to prepare me for my next level and I began my learning journey (books, podcasts, YouTube videos, TedTalks, conferences, etc.)

Step 3   I set the appropriate goals to be sure that they were specific, measurable, achievable, realistic, and time bound (S.M.A.R.T.)

Step 4   I secured several mentors--people who had done what I wanted to do and who had been successful at it. I also ensured that they were willing to share that information without reservation.

Step 5   I got my financial house in order. For me it included paying down debts, saving money, changing my lifestyle, enhancing my credit, and establishing a plan that would enable me to finance my dreams and goals while still being able to pay my bills for the first year.

Step 6   I spent time building my self-confidence, courage, and overcoming my fears and limiting beliefs. I also surrounded myself with a strong network of trusted advisors.

Develop Your Own Exit Strategy

Using the example of how I developed by exit strategy, now develop your own.

Step 1

_____

_____

_____

Step 2

_____

_____

_____

Step 3

_____

_____

_____

Step 4

_____

_____

_____

Step 5

_____

_____

_____

Step 6

_____

_____

_____

Takeaways

If we are ever to get beyond our "What if?" questions, release the limits, and realize our dreams, we have to take those first steps—make the decision to jump, calculate the cost, and devise a plan.

Scan this QR code to listen to a personal message from me.

Chapter 8
The Payoffs of Living Beyond
"What If?"

"True success and happiness come from the highest, truest, and most complete version of ourselves and the purpose for which we were born.."

 **Reflection Exercise**

1. What do you think will be a few of the most invaluable payoffs to Living Beyond "What if" for you?

_____

_____

_____

_____

_____

_____

_____

_____

_____

_____

_____

Chapter 8 Takeaways: Dreams Still Get Disrupted

Even on this side of my journey, yes, I still experience setbacks and unexpected disruptions. This is called life. Amid these disruptions I have come to realize that no matter how much you think you have evolved, life has a way of continuing to test you and throw you curve balls. When that happens, you have to be ready to duck or strike back. I have come to understand that life is not what happens to you; it's what you do with what happens to you. And the lessons, the wisdom, and the successes that come from your experiences are not to be stored in a bottle, put on a shelf, or hidden under the covers. They shouldn't be the best-kept secret. They should be shared with others as testimonials that bring hope, light, and fulfillment. Today I share my stories all over the world with people from various backgrounds, cultures, beliefs, languages, and personalities. They seem to resonate across all ages, stages, and phases of life.

As you conclude this Reflection Journal you've taken the time to:

1. **Reflect on the dreams/imaginations you had as a kid**
2. **Identify the reasons for procrastinating and list those things you procrastinate on the most**
3. **Work on avoiding being stuck in present bias**
4. **Dismantle your disempowering "What if?" questions and are working on replacing them with empowering responses**
5. **Learn to face your fears head on**
6. **Plan your ME-TREAT**
7. **Discover your purpose, and formulate your Life Plan**
8. **Reevaluate your relationships and identified your personal board of advisers**
9. **Develop the courage to jump and grow your wings on the way down**

Scan this QR code to listen to a personal message from me.

Notable Quotables

1. Life is 10% of what happens to you, and 90% of how you respond to what happens to you.
2. Don't just go through it, grow through it.
3. There are only two kinds of fears that are born with: the fear of falling and the fear of a loud sound. All other fears are learned.
4. You're either living your dreams or living your fears.
5. Failure is an option. Learn to fail fast and fail forward.
6. Failing at something doesn't make you a failure, nor does and making mistakes make you the mistake.
7. What you resist will persist.
8. If you don't learn from your mistakes you are doomed to repeat them.
9. Life is like taking a test or exam at school. If you pass it you move to the next level. If you fail it you have to repeat the class.
10. Opportunities never look like opportunities. They come brilliantly disguised as problems and challenges, awaiting a solution.
11. Your dream must be bigger than your fear.
12. It's one thing to be alive, it's another thing to be living.
13. In life, not everything is meant to be forever—some things have an expiration date, and we must discern when that time arrives.
14. You cannot conquer what you aren't willing to confront.
15. We create our own reality by the way we speak.
16. True success and happiness come from fulfilling the highest, truest, and most complete version of ourselves and the purpose that we were born for.
17. Even when you've had a phenomenal year of success you cannot park there and become complacent.
18. What lies behind you and what lies ahead of you are tiny compared to what lies within you.

19. Purpose is so personal that no one else has been designed to do what you were born to do.
20. The only thing that is keeping us from getting what we want are the messages we keep telling ourselves and those that we keep believing.
21. Relationships are the new currency.
22. Imagination is the most powerful tool that we have.
23. Get out of your head so that you can step into your greatness.
24. Become a producer and not a procrastinator.
25. Nobody likes to follow a parked car.
26. We are the sum total of our thoughts, beliefs, and confessions.
27. Most people die at age 30 and don't get buried until age 85.
28. Procrastination will never allow you to live the life you've always dreamed. It is an epidemic that can only be cured and corrected if the underlying root causes are discovered and conquered.
29. If fear is a learned response, we can unlearn and relearn a different response.
30. It's not just what you know, or who you know, but what they know about you.

About the Author

Dr. Shirley Davis is a sought-after global workforce expert, and is president and CEO of SDS Global Enterprises, a strategic development solutions firm that specializes in human resources strategy; talent management; leadership effectiveness; culture transformation; and diversity, equity, and inclusion. Dr. Davis has over twenty years of experience in a variety of senior executive leadership roles in Fortune 100 & 50 corporations and in her last role, served as vice president of global diversity and inclusion and workforce strategies for the world's largest human resources association, the Society for Human Resource Management. Her work has been featured by the Wall Street Journal, NBC's Today Show, USA Today, CBS News, Fox News, CNN.com, Fast Company, CEOWorld Magazine, Harvard Business Review, and many others. In May 2022, her story was featured on the front page of Oprah Daily.
As a result of her contributions and expertise in the HR, Leadership, and DEI fields, she was inducted into Inclusion Magazine's Hall of Fame for Diversity, Equity, and Inclusion in November 2021, and in August 2022 in Nashville, TN she received The Golden Gavel Award which is Toastmasters International's highest and most prestigious award given to only one person each year. Additionally, she was nominated for Forbes 2021 Women 50 Over 50 list and again in 2022.

Dr. Davis has worked in more than 30 countries on 5 continents and delivers more than 100 speeches a year to a wide range of industries, sectors, and sizes, including Fortune 10s-500s corporations, large membership associations and non-profit organizations, and federal, state, and local government agencies. She continues to consult, coach, and train leaders at all levels, including Corporate CEOs, C-Suite executives, Board of Directors. She served on the Board of Directors and the Foundation Board for the National Speakers Association (2017-2021) and led their first-ever NSA DEI Task Force. She is currently a member of the NSA Million Dollar Speakers Group, and a member of the Global Speakers Federation. In 2021, she was named to the national board of the Make-A-Wish Foundation and will serve a four year term. She holds a Bachelor's in Pre-Law, a Master's in Adult Education; a second Master's in Human Resource Management, and a Ph.D. in Business and Organizational Leadership. Dr. Shirley Davis is the author of the recently released book Living Beyond "What If?" Release the Limits and Realize Your Dreams (Berrett-Koehler Publishers, August 10, 2021). She's also the author of Reinvent Yourself: Strategies for Achieving Success in Every Area of Your Life and The Seat: How to Get Invited to the Table When You're Over-Performing but Undervalued. Additionally, she is a popular author for seven LinkedIn Learning courses on Leadership and DEI, and in January 2021 was sought out by another global publishing company--John Wiley & Sons to write the first-ever Diversity, Equity, and Inclusion for Dummies book (released January 10, 2022 as Amazon's #1 New Release in its category and #7 Best Seller).

She is a former Miss District of Columbia National Teenager, Mrs. Oklahoma-America, Ms. Richmond Virginia, Ms. Virginia, and in 2000 she won the national title of Ms. American United States. But among her many accomplishments and titles, the one she holds dearest is "mom" to her daughter, Gabrielle Victoria.

For more information or to book Dr. Shirley Davis for your next event visit her website at www.drshirleydavis.com

Book Dr. Shirley Davis for your next event on one of the following topics from her book:

Living Beyond "WHAT IF?"

- Getting Beyond "What If?": Strategies for Releasing the Limits and Realizing Your Goals and Dreams
- How to Live your Best Life and Why 90% of People Admit That They are Not
- The Importance of an "Exit Strategy": How to Develop One for Every Facet of Your Life
- The Psychology of Present Bias and How it Can Keep You From Realizing Your Dreams
- Relationships are the New Currency: How to Leverage Your Networks and Contacts for Greater Success
- Seven Steps to Becoming Your Most Productive Self
- The Most Common Disempowering "What If?" Questions: How to get Beyond Them and Adopt Empowering Responses
- Jump First and Grow Your Wings on the Way Down—Strategies for Taking Risks and Overcoming Mistakes
- The Power of ME-Treats: Why Everyone Should Take One for Mental Well-Being and Self-Care
- The Golden Cage: How Living in Fear can Cause us to Shut Down and Shut Others Out
- Up Close and Personal with Dr. Davis (How she survived and thrived through near-death experiences, financial bankruptcy, failed relationships, career setbacks and self-imposed fears and insecurities)
- Mastering the Art of Reinvention: Keys to Personal Transformation and Success
- Failure IS an Option: How to Make the Most of Life's Mistakes and Missteps

www.drshirleydavis.com